Critical Thinking:

A Powerful Critical Thinking Guide: 20 Effective Strategies to Improve Critical Thinking and Decision Making Skills

Introduction

I want to thank you and congratulate you for downloading the book, "**Critical Thinking:** *A Powerful Critical Thinking Guide: 20 Effective Strategies to Improve Critical Thinking and Decision Making Skills*".

This book contains proven steps and strategies on how to develop and integrate critical thinking skills into your everyday life and on your worksite. I include in this book

- What is Critical Thinking
- The Roots of Critical Thinking
- Common Factors in Critical Thinking
- Steps to Critical Thinking Decision Making
- How to Incorporate Critical Thinking into your Life
- Strategies for Improving Critical Thinking
- Strategies for Quick and Effective Decision Making
- The Importance of Emotional Intelligence and Critical Thinking
- Steps to the Critical Thinking Process
- 20 Critical Thinking Improvement Exercises

Although this book is not the definitive guide to critical thinking, it will help guide you into practicing and participating in higher thinking.

This book offers exercises for daily critical thinking strengthening, so that you can build on the foundation of reason and logic. There are hints and reminders to help you discard old habits and embrace deeper thinking and the challenges it brings.

Thanks again for downloading this book, I hope you enjoy it!

Table of Contents

Chapter One: What is Critical Thinking?

Critical thinking is the disciplined process of analyzing, evaluating, conceptualizing, synthesizing and applying reasoning, observation, experience and reflection to make decisions based on logic, rather than impulse or emotion. Critical thinking requires evaluation of the purpose, the problem, elimination of the assumptions, evaluation of consequences in the future based on the decision or the outcome, and contextual framework. Critical thinking is related to other modes of thinking such as anthropological thinking, scientific thinking, philosophical thinking, and moral thinking.[1]

Critical thinking has two elements,

1. Information and belief processing competence, and
2. The habit of using those skills to make informed decision for behavior guidance.

Persons who have developed the habit of critical thinking have been determined to be more empathetic, logical, fair-minded, reasonable and rational. They use the tools of analysis to develop a reasonable response to the happenings of their life.

---

[1] (Criticalthinking.org, 2015)

They do not make impulsive decisions that can wreak havoc on society and self. They embody the Socratic principle: *An unexamined life is not worth living.*

The Roots of Critical Thinking

The roots of critical thinking begin with Socrates, 2500 years ago, who noted that persons, when asked to justify their answers to questions, could not give a logical or reasoned response. The responses were based on either emotions or impulse thinking, which is subjective, instead of objective. Socrates noted that only through critical thinking and assessment are we to arrive at a logical, well-examined solution to our problems that is not shallow or impulsive.

Plato continued the teachings of Socrates by promoting examination of our thoughts by self, instead of depending on the forefathers. He suggested that we ask deeply informed questions before accepting the ideas of others, regardless of their societal stature or age.

Thomas Aquinas, in the Middle Ages, added the concept of cross-examination to critical thinking, noting that not all ideas are to be rejected, just those that are without a foundation of reason.

Sir Francis Bacon suggested that proof was a necessary component of critical thinking. He stated that we cannot trust our minds without proof of evidence and observation.

Next to influence critical thinking was Rene Descartes, who challenged assumptions and stated critical thinking would challenge the assumptions of men and be based on a solid foundation of reason.

Sir Isaac Newton suggested tossing aside all the previous thoughts about science and use critical thinking to create verifiable evidence and sound reasoning.

By this point, the examination of thought began to turn inward to self-reflection. As the great thinkers of the nineteenth and twentieth centuries passed on their knowledge, we now have a new threshold of understanding and illumination.

Thinking must be regulated to be effectual, logic must be the foundation for thought, and reasoning should be based on verifiable evidence that has been thoroughly examined for bias. The thinking man is one who is involved in self-examination and reflection to discern any selfish and egotistical tendencies that prevent emotional intelligence.

Chapter Two: Why Choose Critical Thinking?

Everyone thinks in some manner or another. Unfortunately, much of the thinking we do is biased, uninformed, and even prejudiced. However, our quality of life and our purpose in life are directly guided by our thinking habits. If we engage in shallow thinking that is managed by our emotional life, then we will be missing the deep engagement of a life with purpose, reasoning, and meaning.

A critical thinker will engage in logistical, reasonable thoughts and streamline their thoughts and behaviors to align with the critical reasoning. An emotional thinker will have haphazard thoughts and irrational beliefs, which will result in a chaotic life. It is much harder for an emotional thinker to achieve their dreams and goals than a critical thinker. A critical thinker improves their life standards systematically through goals and objectives, adapting their behavior to achieve their goals.

A critical thinker is one who:

- Asks questions about every part of the decision making process
- Looks for relevant information and applies it to the situation, not relying upon opinion or trends,

- Thinks open mindedly when looking for solutions, trying different streams of thought rather than just one source, and
- Communicates with the team to find effective solutions to the problem, not hoarding knowledge or sources, nor discarding evidence that disproves their theories.

Critical thinking is self-monitored, self-examined, self-criticized, and self-determining, allowing the person to contribute to society while remaining their own counsel. Critical thinkers are not swayed by the wind of trends or groups, and do not depend on their elders to do the thinking for them.

What Level Critical Thinker Are You?

Before you delve into critical thinking strategies and skills, use this time to evaluate where you are on the plane of critical thinkers.[2]

Stage 1   The Unreflective Thinker

We are unaware of problems in our thinking that are causing issues in our life. We have no knowledge of how to think, assess, or examine information to determine solutions to a problem. We can repeat information, but we cannot create

---

[2] (Westsidetoastmasters.com, 2015)

logical data. Our decisions are based on emotion, rather than logic. We live in chaos.

Stage 2   The Challenged Thinker

We become aware of problems in our thinking, and realize it may be causing significant problems in our life and our relationships. We realize other people have an easier time with decisions and consequences. We know something is wrong, but do not have the knowledge necessary to know how to fix the problem.

Stage 3   The Beginning Thinker

We are aware that our thinking is flawed and attempt to better ourselves by some discernment in our thinking. We have realized that egocentrism is part of our flawed thinking. We attempt to use logic some of the time in our decision-making.

Stage 4   The Practicing Thinker

We are aware that we need to change the way we think in a systematic and progressive manner. We realize that we have to internalize good thinking skills and practice them routinely. We are beginning to see the inner peace that comes with critical thinking.

Stage 5   The Advanced Thinker

We are utilizing the concepts of critical thinking on a daily basis, regularly examining thoughts for logic, reason, and clarity. We are giving back to the community and participating in a more meaningful way. We are expanding our reading and information venues.

Stage 6   The Accomplished Thinker

We are continually processing and examining our thinking to utilize the higher concepts of critical thinking. We are reading the classics of literature. We are applying critical thinking in all aspects of our lives without prompts to do what is good and right. We have lost the need to feed our ego.

It is important to note that persons are not considered critical thinkers if they do not employ this ability in all aspects and circumstances of their lives. They should be utilizing these concepts as a parent, friend, student, in the workplace, and with their closest peers. If critical thinking is only used in one venue, such as the workplace, then the rest of this person's life will be chaotic, at best. The quality of one's life is derived from character and the practice of reason, logic, and clarity of thought.

Chapter Three: Critical Thinking Habits

Critical thinking is the engagement of self-examination through the thought process. Thoughts are no longer accepted as informative links, but instead, are examined for logic, reasoning, a sound foundation and concept, and future implications. The information flow in our head can be short-circuited at any time by assumptions and emotions, both impulsive forms of knowledge that can hijack our logic and reasoning.

Common Factors in Critical Thinking

Within critical thinking, there will be questions regarding:

- Information and its source
- The ends and means of a situation
- The specific language used to word a question
- The method by which information was collected
- The veracity of the information
- The assumptions inherent in the concepts supplied
- The judgment used to make an assumption
- The implications of the information
- The consequences of using the information
- The reasoning used to conclude the information

So that the information used is examined thoroughly for bias and prejudice before it becomes the foundation for decision-making.

There are also 8 habits the most effective critical thinkers practice, according to Guinn and Williamson of PSP Metrics.[3]

1. They are more interested in getting it right than being right. They are interested in finding the best solution, not being the one to deliver the solution. They are not interested in being the hero or the know-it-all.

2. They avoid rushing in their decision making processes. They weigh all the facts and look to others for verified information, taking all into consideration to arrive at the right conclusion.

3. They do not accept unverified information. They ask questions about the source and the veracity of the information. They gather data from different sources.

4. They stop gathering information when they have enough to make the decision. They don't over-process, second-guess, or over-analyze the situation.

---

[3] (Guinn & Williamson, 2015)

5. They are curious about a wide range of topics and they never stop learning. They manage their day to stay well-informed of the local, national, and world events.

6. They are flexible and consider information from a variety of sources. They learn new technology and rapidly see the advantage of progress.

7. They use critical thinking for self-assessment and reflection. They are also quick to be able to explain their logic and reasoning behind the decision making process. They will change their decision when confronted with a better idea.

8. They have a specific character. They are reflective. They implement change. They think independently. They accept responsibility and look to see how they can improve. They are well-read.

Chapter Four: How to Incorporate Critical Thinking into your Life

There are six skills necessary to incorporate critical thinking into your pattern of thinking. I will include these skills below with a small exercise to practice the critical thinking competency.

Interpretation

Interpretation is the ability to understand the information as it is presented, and in turn, the ability to convey that information accurately to other persons.

- As you continue in the workforce you will be given information by which to discern the goal of a project, the deadline of a writing exercise, or perhaps the blueprint of a building. Having accurate interpretation skills will help you decipher the information and then present the findings to a separate group of people, like investors or the sales staff.

Exercise: List 12 emotions you associate with facial expressions or body language, like someone sitting all hunched over with their arms wrapped together appears to embody rejection. Give your list to a friend and ask them to role play the emotions. Try to correctly guess the emotion as they role play. When you hit one incorrectly, ask them about their portrayal. Were you accurate in the interpretation or were they?

Analysis

Analysis is the ability to assemble nuggets of information and correctly interpret the meaning of the information in a given situation.

- Using analytical skills is an essential business competency because it allows you to think past what is written on the page. If you receive a memo stating the sales force will be moving to Montana, and you are part of the sales force, you should be able to analyze that notice and put your house in order. With analysis, you will know to literally pack your home and get rid of clutter for the company relocation of your department.

Exercise: Analyze the Chinese proverb "*may you live in interesting times*." What is the meaning behind the proverb? What is the mood of the one making the statement? Who could they be addressing? Do they like this person?

Inference

Inference is a conclusion based on the foundation of evidence and information.

- In the business world, inference is used to determine internal conflicts, competitions, and external influences that determine the business decisions of the manager. Inference is understanding what information you have in order to determine where the evidence and reasoning are lacking to fill the big picture.

Exercise: Watch an episode of an older crime show, like Murder She Wrote. Follow the clues given in the story and see if you can determine the bad guy by the clues given. Were you able to find the perpetrator?

Evaluation

Evaluation is the ability to measure the veracity of a person's experience in order to measure the weight the testimony should be given.

- In a business situation, many customers make complaints about products for one reason or another. It is important to know how much weight to give the person that claims there was a foreign object in their sleeve of beef jerky, for example. You will need to be able to ascertain if these are false statements by your evaluation skills.

Exercise: Each time you watch a television commercial you are using evaluation skills when you watch an advertisement for a product. You should be asking yourself, "Is this a credible source?" "Can I trust their judgment?" "How much weight should I give to their testimony?" All of these questions should be at the forefront before you decide to purchase their products.

Explanation

Explanation is the ability to understand what is stated and being able to interpret the information, and appropriately convey it to another concerned party.

- In business, it is very important to be able to impart information accurately and succinctly to the appropriate interested parties. When conveying information, remember not everyone needs to hear all the details to gain an understanding of the situation.

Exercise: Practice discernment by explaining an idea (that has three parts) to both a first grader and a college graduate. Note the differences in your vocabulary and focus of the explanation. Have both of them repeat back to your their understanding of the idea. Do not talk for more than two minutes. This will give you editing skills also.

Self-Regulation

Self-regulation is the ability to understand what you think and how you determine your results.

- In a business situation, this is most helpful when you realize that your method of communication may not be adequate for the customer at hand, so you refer them to someone with the same type of communication skills or someone more knowledgeable about the product.

Exercise: Learn to self-regulate by identifying personal bias while at work. Write down 10 reasons you deserve a promotion. How many of the answers were related to self-interest instead of company interests? Rewrite them now focusing only on the company interests.

Chapter Five: Stages of Critical Thinking Used in Analysis

Here are three stages to help you critically analyze a problem efficiently.

1.   Identify the purpose of the decision or the goal of the informative report.

When you identify the purpose of the decision, every other decision within the collective should be moving to the culmination of the stated goal. If you are hoping to increase your market share of wrench sales, this is not the time to introduce a new product, like nuts and bolts. If your stated goal is the increase of wrench sales, then each decision for advertising dollars and the sales force staff attention should be directed towards increasing that one sales category, wrenches. Do not diversify and split the attention to other products.

2.   Examine your internal prejudices.

It is common to view a problem from your personal perspective with a few blinders in the way. Limiting yourself to your own point of view can lead to overspending, ignoring good information, and making bad business decisions.

Ask yourself what you base your assumptions on? What do you know about the workers and the situation and what do you assume about the case? Are you projecting your feelings onto another person's answers? Have you tainted the information because you don't like the presenter? All of these are crucial questions so that you can make informed business decisions separate from your internal prejudices. Articulate your thoughts aloud. Can you hear bias in them?

3. Assess the implications of your decision.

Look at all areas and everyone involved. In today's workplace, your decision to take the wrench manufacturing overseas to reduce manufacturing costs will reduce the domestic workforce. Do you have replacement jobs for the domestic employees? Will you have to incur the cost of unemployment taxes, training, or workforce development here? Will this offset the profit from the overseas move?

Chapter Six: Strategies for Improving Quick and Effective Decision Making

Utilizing the OODA Loop in Decision Making

Using the OODA loop that was utilized by the United States Air Force in air combat missions, we break down the loop into a four-stage decision making process:[4]

Observe - note what the information says, gather from all sources possible

Orient - analyze your information to update your current situation

Decide - determine the correct path to meet your goal

Act - implement your decision as soon as possible

While in the observation mode, look to see how this information directly affects you and your department. Will this mean that you must cut employees? Do you need to redirect your resources? Is there any area that I predicted accurate results? Was I way off in my predictions somewhere?

While in the orientation mode, be aware of the these things that influence your decision making process:

- Cultural heritage
- Race and roles in your community
- Past experience in a similar situation

---

[4] (Mindtools.com, 2015)

- New information not yet processed
- Your personal ability to put aside prejudices
- Your ability to analyze

While in the decision mode, remember to be fluid. Look at each piece of information as it is gathered and add it to the current equation. Keep timely with the results of your situation. Don't base decisions on stale statistics.

In the action mode, start the process over again. This is a cycle, not a linear endpoint.

Systematic Decision Making

There are seven critical tools needed to effectively make decisions. Using these tools to assess your situation will assure that you have not overlooked important information needed for your final solution to the workplace problem.

1. Create an open environment where each contribution is valued and given the same attention.
2. Investigate the problem in detail to determine what is the originating issue, or if you are just examining the symptoms of the issue
3. Brainstorm ideas in the group, and ask people to write solutions on pieces of paper that are read aloud to the group for consideration. Many times persons in a group can be hesitant to contribute for fear of ridicule. Having

people write solutions on paper will bring out more than one good idea for the project at hand.

4. Explore all the options for the feasibility, risks and outcomes of each scenario.

5. Select the best option for a solution. Try to reach a consensus within the group, but do not let the group turn into a popularity contest.

6. Evaluate the chosen solution. Look again at the risks, costs, feasibility, and projected outcomes. Look for unintended consequences.

7. Implement your solution and take action. Discuss the decision making process with those involved to attract more interest.[5]

---

[5] (Mindtools.com, 2015)

Chapter Seven: Emotional Intelligence and Critical Thinking

Emotional intelligence is the ability to filter emotions from the process of critical decision making. A person with a high proficiency in emotional intelligence would make rational decisions based on feelings, but more so on the information and reasoning in the situation.

Critical thinking is the vehicle by which we judge our emotional life, lest we fall into the trap of decision making by emotional investment. If we analyze the situation according to the facts and information derived from a neutral source, we are more likely to make a strong decision that will maintain our goals. If we assess a situation based on our emotional filters, we are likely to draw a wrong conclusion and choose a course of action that is detrimental to our long term goals.

When our decision making process includes feelings and emotions, we tend to gravitate toward selfishness. Are not the first words learned by a toddler, "It's mine!" This is an example of the selfish nature of humanity. Throughout our lives we make decisions based on our best interests, as we see them. We want to think of ourselves as generous, kind, thoughtful, considerate, but in reality we act in manipulation to get what we want when we want it. Emotions that are associated with selfishness include shallowness, defensiveness, arrogance, anger, self-aggrandizement, and self-promotion.

Persons that are critical thinkers, and emotionally intelligent, will choose to reach beyond petty selfishness to embrace higher values. Those higher values are for the good of the business, or the good of society, or even to the good of mankind.

Benchmarks of Emotional Intelligence

There are five benchmarks of emotional intelligence according to Daniel Goleman, author of the best selling books, *Emotional Intelligence: Why It Can Matter More Than IQ* and *Working With Emotional Intelligence:*[6]

- **Self-Awareness**
- Emotionally intelligent people know who they are and what their boundaries and limits need to be. They understand their role and their impact on the surrounding team. A good judge of emotion intelligence is how the person receives constructive criticism.

---

[6] (Simmons, 2015)

- **Self-Regulation**
- Emotionally intelligent people can control their emotions and respond in a professional manner at all times. They may have anger but they will not exhibit anger in a given situation.

- **Motivation**
- Emotionally intelligent people are ambitious but not driven. They are generally optimistic and resourceful, looking for solutions to problems beyond the stereotypical response.

- **Empathy**
- Emotionally intelligent people can see the other side of the coin and respond empathetically. They understand a sick child or a sick headache can undermine even the best of decisions.

- **People Skills**
- Emotionally intelligent people have good people skills. They don't tell hurtful jokes, they don't tease unmercifully, and they don't make broad, underhanded remarks to other employees. They support their staff and make contributions to the team, regardless of their position of authority.

Six Steps to Increasing Your Emotional Intelligence

Each of us wants to be emotionally intelligent, mature, and aware of our feelings and thoughts, and able to control them in the business environment. Somehow the emotions will creep in and hijack the best of days, turning it upside down in a whirlwind of negative feelings. This control can be obtained by working the six steps delineated below.

1. Reduce the negative emotions in your life. Instead of assuming the bad of a situation, think of alternatives to place the good on the forefront. Yes, you had a flat tire today BUT it gave you an opportunity to ride to work with your spouse, sharing a vehicle, time together, and saving fuel. Widen your perspective to include opportunities for change.

    a. Reduce your personalization of issues. If a team member doesn't return your call, it is like more their issue than yours. Instead of thinking, this team member doesn't like/trust/respect me; place the issue where it belongs. The team member is overwhelmed with their workload and doesn't have time for one more call at the end of the day.

    b. Reduce your fear of rejection. We all want to be loved. We all want to be accepted. Instead of placing your fears on the doorstep of vulnerability, neutralize your fears by allowing for more than one choice. If you are sending a manuscript to be published, send the manuscript to more than one place. Give yourself opportunities to be accepted, instead of using one publisher control over your destiny.

2. When under stress, use cooling strategies to buy time and relax yourself. Do aerobic exercises for a few minutes or splash cool water on your face. Both will relax and reorient your thinking.

3. Learn to be assertive and express your emotions when the situation calls for disclosure. Practice stating sentences like, "I feel discarded when you abruptly change the subject when I offer a solution to the problem at issue."

4. Stay proactive, not reactive in the face of a difficult challenge. Do not allow your emotions dictate your response.

5. Nurture the ability to bounce back from adversity. No matter what the circumstance, never give up, and never stop trying. Michael Jordan said, *"I've missed more than 9000 shots in my career. I've lost almost 300 games. 26 times, I've been trusted to take the game winning shot and missed. I've failed over and over and over again in my life. And that is why I succeed."*[7]

---

[7] (Ni, 2015)

6. Learn to express your innermost thoughts and feelings to another person in a close relationship. Learn to nurture another person while nurturing yourself.

Chapter Eight: The Path to Critical Thinking

Build on a foundation of critical thinking exercises. If you are not familiar with critical thinking basics, start with the first item on the list and practice it for the day. Each day practice the example for the day, and go back and include the examples from the day before. In this way, you are creating a foundation of higher thinking skills.

If on one day you feel confused or that you did not thoroughly understand the concept, use the skill for a second day until your feel accomplished in the task.

- Think deeply to connect all the dots in the puzzle. Do not just skim the surface of the issue at hand.
- Ask questions that clarify your information. Don't dismiss something because you don't like the messenger or the message.
- Use research and evidence to support your thinking, instead of opinion.
- Analyze a situation, reason out a solution, and evaluate the outcome of your solution.
- Go deeper. Interpret the information beyond the shallow surface.

- Consider diverse forms of information; do not limit yourself to one source or one form.
- Make a point of solving important and complex problems.
- Evaluate all your options before coming to a solution to a problem.
- Focus on the details of a situation to analyze the clear meaning of the complexities.
- Apply reasoning to all your solutions.
- Use objective criteria to analyze information. Don't let your bias or ego get in the way.
- Follow known problem solving steps
  - ☐ Define the problem
  - ☐ Focus on the problem, not the symptoms of the problem
  - ☐ Brainstorm solutions
  - ☐ Pick the best solution
  - ☐ Analyze the potential outcome
  - ☐ Act upon the solution
  - ☐ Analyze the results

Think independently first, then think with a group to design solutions to advanced problems. Consider all the contributions equal, with merit. Consider all options that are conveyed in the group. Eliminate solutions with logic and reasoning, not with emotion or bias. Implement the solution by utilizing everyone in the group. Contribute your solution as just one of many. Maintain the group decision. Lose your ego.

Chapter Nine: Six Steps in the Critical Thinking Process for the Beginner

When you have completed the six steps in the critical thinking process, you have proven that you have absorbed the information and are able to derive a solution based on logic and reason.

1. The first step in the critical thinking process is to demonstrate that you have learned the basic facts and information regarding the project or subject. You can do this by listing and identifying the main parts of the project or topic. Do this numerically on a piece of paper as a mind exercise. Do you see more than one issue? Good, you are using your analytical skills.

2. The second step in the critical thinking process is to demonstrate knowledge of the project. Can you summarize the project in one sentence? Can you explain it to a group of people that have no previous information regarding the project? Can you explain it to a first-grader? What about to a college graduate? You should be able to simplify the project terms and expand upon the requirements as the situations needs.

3. The third step in the critical thinking process is to apply the knowledge you have acquired in steps one and two. Can you use this knowledge in another similar situation? Can you see parallels to other workplace problems?

4. The fourth step in the critical thinking process is the ability to analyze the information by comparing and contrasting known facts and ideas. Look for solutions inside and outside of the box. Explore all possibilities. Think traditionally, and then think creatively.

5. The fifth step in the critical thinking process is applying the information to your known knowledge to possibly create something new. Take what you know and what you were given and combine them to create a solution to the problem.

6. The sixth step in the critical thinking process is to evaluate the solution, explain your thinking processes, and implement the best solution, assessing its worth.

Chapter Ten: 20 Critical Thinking Improvement Strategies

Exercises to Alter Your Thinking

There are many strategies that can be used to alter your thinking and develop critical thinking skills. We have chosen these 20 for practice to improve your decision making processes.

1.   Use your wasted time in concrete ways. Assess how much time you really spend piddling, daydreaming, and playing games, etc. Use this time to a better advantage. Assess your day and the decisions you made. Could any of them used the extra minutes you spent whiling away? Did you do anything today to progress toward your long term goals? Did you act on your belief system? Was there a time that your emotional processes changed a decision? Was this for the better or worse? If I do this (a repeat of today) for two weeks, will I move closer toward my goals?

2.   Pick one problem to work on for the day. Think about this issue in your spare time. Write down solutions to the problem. Write down steps for implementation. Can you solve

the problem with a satisfactory solution that takes into account your information from all informed sources?

3.   Develop an awareness of the higher thinking standards. Begin to internalize these standards by applying one a day for a period of time. Start with clarity. Look at the issue objectively, without the filter of presupposition and bias. Next use precision. Be precise in reporting what you see and what you have learned. Accuracy is next. Then look at depth, logic, reason, and the breadth of your knowledge on a given subject. Learn to improve your information by doing extensive research on your own time, not piddling away the time in entertainments. Practice stating your position, elaborating on the decision making process, clarifying your decision and using examples from situations to explain your position to Clearly reveals your position in four points.

4.   Keep a thinking journal with these categories:

Situation, describe an emotionally significant situation.

Response, what did you specifically do in response to the stated situation?

Analysis, what was really going on in the situation?

Self-assessment, what would you differently now, when looking back?

5.   Practice reshaping your character to become the higher thinker. Choose one trait, for example, courage to embody each month. Practice everyday to overcome your fears and prejudices to become more courageous. What does courageous mean to you? How will it look on a regular basis? What will you stop doing in order to become more courageous? Notice when your ego gets in the way of your higher thinking. Note when fear overcomes faith in the process, person, or event.

6.   Deal with your ego. Begin to notice your egocentric ways. Watch your thinking by observing things like; under what circumstances do I tend to become irritable? Do I say or do manipulative or irrational things to get my way?

7.   Reform the way you think to have a better attitude. Turn your negative assessment into positive thinking by reorienting your attitude. Form an attitude of gratitude instead of a sour frown in reaction to information. Turn mistakes into learning opportunities. Turn rejection into critical assessment of a situation. Apply the point of constructive criticism and lose the attitude of dejection.

8.   Touch your emotional core and evaluate how it affects your decision making. Ask yourself what is really happening when you feel fear or resentment in the workplace? Look at your emotional base and determine where the loneliness is

located, where the hurt may be, and how you may be projecting these emotions in the workplace.

9.   Analyze how group think affects your life. Do you allow your peer group to influence your choices for your future? Do you determine what you will do based on what they will perceive? Higher critical thinking is all about making positive decisions for yourself, without the emotional influence of others. Engaging in higher thinking means leaving peer pressure behind. Step out on your own firm foundation to become the strong person of logic and reason you wish to portray.

10.   Learn to read critically. When you read information, such as the newspaper, ask yourself these questions to evaluate what you have learned.

Why was it written?

To whom?

Where was it written?

When was it written?

By whom?

Is it logical?

Does it present a clear argument?

Is the evidence from different sources?

Is the evidence credible?

Is the evidence from a trusted authority?

What was the purpose of the piece?

Did they persuade you with logic or pull at your emotions?

Was it written from more than one perspective?

Was there a voice eliminated from the piece?

11.   Read a new book a week and evaluate the book. Apply critical thinking to the book. What was the book about? Who were the main characters? Why do you think the author wrote the book? Email the author and ask, because you may be surprised. What is the setting? What is the timeframe? What was a good lesson in the book? What parts did you not like?

12.   Assess your peer group by questioning their higher thinking skills. Ask a specific question you have well researched and ask their opinion of the issue. Pick something nonpolitical and non controversial, but something that takes thought and consideration. Try to start a discussion over the issue. Bring up logical reasoning and use critical thinking skills and observe how they respond. Do they brush you off? Do they joke and criticize? Does anyone give a measured response? Are these friends helping you in accomplishing your goals or hurting you by holding you back with their emotional immaturity? Carefully evaluate why you have chosen this group of friends?

13.   Change your current thinking patterns with this exercise. Write down every negative thing about your life you can consider in your current situation. Don't write down past events because you can't change the past. You can only deal with the present to help you claim the future for your opportunities. Have you listed all the bad things in your life? Now write a positive response beside it. Are you short of money? Then you have opportunities for growth by getting a second job. Do you have major health problems? You are still living, breathing and able to contribute to the world. Did someone say something mean to you? Examine the statement for truth. If it is true, consider why you act this way. If it is a lie, discard it and analyze why they act in a mean way.

14.   Deepen your thinking. Watch the nightly news at 6:00 p.m. Write down the key points from the news broadcast. What were the issues in the world today? What do you know about the key points? Research the facts; know where you stand on the issues of the day. Derive your answers from research and logic, not from an easily dismissed uninformed opinion that was made by a talking head.

15.   Learn to listen to other people's opinions. You are not the only informed voice in the room. Practice active listening by restating the opinion back to the speaker. They will be thrilled you heard their point and you will retain the

information better. Write down their points and then research a conflicting point of view. Engage the person in a rational conversation comparing and contrasting their view with your research. Go beyond the surface factors and dig into the deeper ideas.

16.   Assess the ideas you see in Social Media. At first the idea may seem to have merit, but look further to see if it is a verified fact. Every day there is some kind of meme on social media that states someone has done something offensive to somebody. Instead of taking the gossip at face value, and spreading the gossip to another person, evaluate what you will do with the information. Will it be edifying to the other person? Will it build up your friend? Will it be honorable to discuss with your employer? Is this something you would want your children overhearing? Assess what you are doing with social media. Are you using it to build your character? Are you using it to accomplish your personal goals?

17.   Write a 5 year plan. Start with 5 years out. Really think about where you want to be and what you want to be doing. How will you accomplish this goal? Break it into 5 year increments. Let's use that you want to be financially solvent enough to purchase your own home. You need to save $20,000 for a down payment. This is a savings of $4,000 a year, or $334.00 per month. How will you save that much? If

you turn off cable, you might be able to save $100 a month. If you pick up a second job, at minimum wage you can make $400 a month working approximately 20 extra hours a week. Does your employer offer overtime? Brainstorm the ways that you can accomplish your goal. Consider all avenues.

18.   Examine diverse points of view to put yourself in someone else's perspective. Do you think we have an immigrant issue in the United States? Start from the beginning and research our policies on immigration. What are the quotas for each country? What does the immigrant derive from citizenship? What does citizenship entitle someone to receive? Anything? Where are the roadblocks? Why are the people leaving their country? Look at the issue from the immigrant point of view. Then research solutions. Don't assume you know all the answers; look closely at the questions involved.

19.   Pick a problem you have looming. Now make a reasoned decision about the problem. Make a mind map or a flow chart determining the consequences of your decision. Try to anticipate all the ramifications of your intended actions, not just the immediate consequences. What will this cost in terms of income? What will it cost in terms of friendships? Will it affect your family peace? Will it use more resources than it will gain? Will it affect your employment? Lifestyle? Cost of living?

20.	Choose to be well-informed. Read the classical literature. The books are there because the ideas have stood the test of time. Evaluate the book as to why it is considered a classic. Keep up to date and informed about current events, local, national, and international. Make sure your opinions are informed and relevant to the conversations around you. Observe the successful leaders in your organization. Pick one characteristic to emulate to increase your learning skills. Teach yourself a new skill or hobby. Don't waste your time sitting in an armchair watching a boob tube. Spend your life learning.

Chapter Eleven: Digging a Little Deeper

Expose yourself to bigger challenges and deeper questions. Watch debates that are televised to examine the examples of rational thinking. Would you have picked the same ideas upon which to expound? Which position would you have taken? Who said what in the debate? Was the argument based on reasoning and logic, or an emotional outburst? Who do you think won the debate and why? What did you learn about debating? Could you identify the different elements of critical thinking?

Socrates said, "*The unexamined life is not worth living*." What did he mean? How do you see his statement in relation to your life and practices? Can you see where egocentric thoughts lead to a life of dissolution? Do you agree with Socrates? If he were here today, what would you ask him? If the life is unexamined, to what standard is one accountable?

Begin the practice of reflective thinking. Go into a quiet room and think about your day. What were the highlights of the day? What were the things you would rather have not happened? Is there any decision you made that you regret? Can you change the circumstances now? Was there information unavailable so that you were lacking in full knowledge before you made your decision. Can you rectify this issue? Rate your thinking skills for the day from 1-10. What stopped you from receiving a 10? Are you working on improving your critical thinking skills? Have you stopped trying to accomplish your goals?

Learn to think for yourself. No matter how brilliant your friends or family, they don't know what is best for you, you are the author of your book and the captain of your soul. For you to make the informed decisions for direction in your life to accomplish your goals, you need to have a strong voice in the community and be able to articulate your goals and purpose. Developing this strong voice is the essence of critical thinking. Learn to examine yourself fearlessly to remove the pettiness and shallowness from your character. Try to remove all semblance of ego from your life. Find a higher purpose. Replace your character weaknesses with strength, humility, courage, bravery, and determination.

Practice everyday emulating the ideals from which you desire to form your character. Expecting to wake up tomorrow as a critical thinker that is emotionally mature, and also habitually making informed decisions, is not likely to happen without the application of practice. Be consistent about your self-improvement program. Utilize the ideas in this book and then consult another one. Take care of your health. Eat healthy, nutritious foods and then exercise daily. Make sure you are clean every day. Bathe, Shave, and groom your hair. Wear clean clothing that is modest and in good repair. Make your home clean and inviting. Invite guests in for stimulating conversations about world events. Develop a mature mind-set. Expand your friendships to stretch beyond preset boundaries. Invite new people into your circle of influence. Examine life from a different perspective. Choose to be great, to have brilliant ideas, and to make mature, affirming decisions.

References

Criticalthinking.org,. (2015). *Defining Critical Thinking*. Retrieved 2 November 2015, from http://www.criticalthinking.org/pages/defining-critical-thinking/766

Guinn, S., & Williamson, G. (2015). *Eight Habits of Effective Critical Thinkers. American Management Association*. Retrieved 3 November 2015, from http://www.amanet.org/training/articles/Eight-Habits-of-Effective-Critical-Thinkers.aspx

Mindtools.com,. (2015). *How to Make Decisions: Making the Best Possible Choices*. Retrieved 3 November 2015, from https://www.mindtools.com/pages/article/newTED_00.htm

Mindtools.com,. (2015). *OODA Loops: Understanding the Decision Cycle*. Retrieved 2 November 2015, from https://www.mindtools.com/pages/article/newTED_78.htm

Ni, P. (2015). *How to Increase Your Emotional Intelligence — 6 Essentials. Psychology Today*. Retrieved 3 November 2015, from https://www.psychologytoday.com/blog/communication-success/201410/how-increase-your-emotional-intelligence-6-essentials

Simmons, K. (2015). *Emotional Intelligence: What Smart Managers Know- Articles - Resources - ASAE.Asaecenter.org*. Retrieved 3 November 2015, from http://www.asaecenter.org/Resources/articledetail.cfm?ItemNumber=13040

Westsidetoastmasters.com,. (2015). *Stages of Development of Critical Thinking*. Retrieved 3 November 2015, from http://westsidetoastmasters.com/resources/thinking_tools/ch05.html

Conclusion

Thank you again for downloading this book!

I hope this book was able to help you to begin the self-examination and reflection that leads to critical thinking.

The next step is to practice the critical thinking exercises in this book to enable you to incorporate critical thinking as your lifestyle and daily habit.

Finally, if you enjoyed this book, then I'd like to ask you for a favor, would you be kind enough to leave a review for this book on Amazon? It'd be greatly appreciated!

Thank you and good luck!

20370097R10032

Printed in Poland
by Amazon Fulfillment
Poland Sp. z o.o., Wrocław